Brand, by Design

Seen, Heard, Loved.

How to define what makes you unique and build a wildly- aligned, scroll-stopping brand that'll get you seen, heard and loved by your dream clients

Rosie Wilkins

Copyright © 2023 by Rosie Wilkins

All rights reserved.

No part of this book may be reproduced in any form or by any electronic or mechanical means, including information storage and retrieval systems, without written permission from the author, except for the use of brief quotations in a book review.

Contents

1. Introduction — 5
2. Falling out over fonts — 9
3. Business, Brand, Branding — 19
4. No new messages — 23
5. Think, then do — 29
6. Your Story — 34
7. What's it all for? — 40
8. Scroll-Stopping Visuals — 50
9. Come work with me — 69

Acknowledgments — 75

Chapter 1
Introduction

'BY DESIGN'

phrase/adverb

As a result of a plan; intentionally

Synonyms: intentionally, on purpose, deliberately

'ALIGNMENT'

noun

The process of honouring our core values

Before we get into things, I'd like to preface this little book by saying that this is by no means a full resource when it comes to building your brand. We have 7,000(ish) words and I want to make the most of it, so I'll try and keep things as direct, valuable and to the point as I can for you, but this isn't always a bad thing. Information overload can stall creativity and productivity in the same way a lack of knowledge can so try and think of this as a 'need to know' book.

But first, let me introduce myself and give you some backstory on me...

I am Rosie. Or Rose; whichever floats your boat. I'm a mum of two little girls and when I'm not in the studio you'll probably find me in Starbucks sipping on an Americano, mooching round the Range or B&M, or out with the kids at some kind of Dinosaur related event.

I'm the literal blueprint for a Leo, an introvert and (if you're into Human Design) a 6/2 Emotional Manifestor (lord knows I love a nap). I LOVE to laugh. I think laughing and sleeping are likely my 2 favourite activities and I'm totally the person who often can't finish my own joke because I'm already laughing too hard. If you've ever messaged me, you'll understand how hard writing this book was because I usually end every sentence with an emoji 😉 .

When I was young, my dad was self employed and my mum worked freelance, so my example of a working life was very much a flexible one and I knew when I grew up I wanted to work for myself - I just had zero clue what I might actually do!

Through school I dreamed of being a graphic designer, but it took me until I was 30 (thanks to a less than supportive design teacher) to actually follow through on that dream and believe in myself enough to use those skills, but I'll be honest - I've not looked back since!

I'm super visual, and like to keep things simple and broken down into bitesize chunks. I can't bear meetings for the sake of meetings, and would rather remove all the fluff and get straight to the point (something I think my clients value in my approach).

My philosophy is that we get one life, and we ALL deserve to spend that time doing something we love, with the people we care about most and in order to do these things, we need to build a business that serves us as well as our clients. This is where me, you and this little book come in!

Chapter 2
Falling out over fonts

I didn't always have the control over my life and work that I do now, and actually, this is where my experience in branding begins; after I had my first daughter, Millie back in 2013. I'd wanted to be a graphic designer all through school but despite doing pretty well in my studies my confidence was knocked by a not-so-great design tutor who told me that I didn't have a good grasp of the subject and then told me I'd likely fail the course (spoiler alert - I didn't fail - not even a little bit).

We lived in a little area of Devon where the term 'graphic designer' would have felt foreign to most people. Following that dream would have meant moving to the city and my total lack of self belief meant I put this dream on the back burner.

When Millie arrived some years later, I was working for a holiday home company in my little hometown of Dartmouth in Devon. I took my maternity leave but had zero clue of the size of the cost of childcare and so was only able to go back to my job part-time. After several meetings, advice from an employment solicitor and a visit from the HR department I was granted my part-time hours and not long after my return I was shifted into the role of Marketing Assistant.

I finally got a taste of actually doing the thing I had wanted to do this whole time! I got to create and design adverts for actual newspapers and magazines - I got to create printed flyers and brochures - I got to organise events and campaigns... This was brilliant! They even flew me up North somewhere to visit head office and meet the wider corporate marketing team! How cool was this?

We found though that after paying the nursery fees each month things weren't connecting and there was still too much month left at the end of the money. I knew I needed to bring in more and ended up reaching out to a network marketing company as it was the only thing I could think of to supplement my income without creating more childcare costs.

Network marketing taught me a tonne about who I was, how to use social media to build a business and how important branding was. Sure, I was working in marketing, but this brand was already established - MY brand was not, and I was competing against thousands of other people who had the same products at the same prices. I learnt quickly that if I was going to stand out, I needed to leverage the only thing I had that made my business unique - ME! People were buying from me because they knew me and they trusted me. I just needed to be myself; but while this sounds simple, what the last eight years have taught me is that this is not the case and showing up in your default settings - on purpose - can be the stumbling block that stops a business from getting off the ground.

Around eleven months after I'd begun building my network marketing business, I went to work one morning to receive an email regarding a font I had changed on the company website. When I visited the corporate team, we had flagged that one of the font styles used on the website was not actually one of our brand fonts and so we changed it. It was quite a minuscule change (so small I could probably flick between the two mid-sentence and most people wouldn't notice) but this email would have you thinking I'd gone ahead and just deleted the whole site. I was to be 'publicly flogged' (her actual words, not mine) for my actions and this email was CC'd to all the lovely people I'd spent the day meeting at corporate.

That was the morning I wrote my resignation and a month later I went full-time in my network marketing business. In hindsight, I'm not sure why I was kind enough to work out my notice - it's not like I needed the reference, but I guess I was a little softer back then compared to how I am now.

Anyway, in the two years after this, me and my little team (I say little, we were around 500 at this point) sold somewhere in the region of half a million pounds in products just by showing up as ourselves! We were having fun - doing things our way and our genuine passion and excitement was contagious. People wanted IN and wanted to be in our space. I can't even tell you we were doing anything particularly special, but when you build your personal brand by showing up unapologetically as yourself and allowing people to connect with you, this is where magic can happen.

I was even able to team up with two other leaders and leverage the brands and influence we had built to run and grow an annual training event! The second year we had more than 250 attendees and people travelled from all over the country - this will always be one of my proudest days.

Armed with the ability now to build a business on social media, I decided in 2018 it was time to let go of what my design tutor had said and finally become a designer. My partner, Guy, had joined a fantasy football league and they needed a poster - I was super excited to help and mocked something up for them. Someone jokingly asked if he'd paid someone to do it and honestly, the rest is history. With my tiny 11-inch Macbook and an Adobe subscription I made myself a website, and a Facebook account and off I went.

M Design Co was born and boy did this teach me a lot.

I knew design. This I could do.

The software was another story

And I no longer had a team or a sponsor to go to for help or bounce ideas off.

I was on my own in a brand-new industry, celebrating because I'd learned how to draw a circle in Adobe Illustrator!

My lack of experience meant I came in lowballing myself with prices. I was charging logos out at £29 for my first few months. £29! I can tell you now there is ZERO money to be made at that price and definitely no work/life balance.

After working all the hours, hitting burnout, constantly being on my phone, and getting frustrated over revisions because I hadn't put any boundaries in place I knew I needed to raise my rates.

But how?

Slowly over the next few months, I began to put my prices up; celebrating each time someone booked with me at the new price!

Then I fell pregnant with Evalyn and everything changed.

She arrived two weeks before the first lockdown hit and I was suddenly faced with a new baby, home-schooling my then 6-year-old, not being able to leave the house, recovering from childbirth, my partner working from home upstairs and trying to keep my head generally above water and everyone alive and fed.

Then there was work to think about.

There was zero chance I could work the same hours I had done before. I needed to be able to make more money in less time, but I also wanted to be able to make more impact for my clients.

So, I invested what I could into a brand strategy course and OMG it opened my eyes!

This was all I already knew about branding but wildly intensified.

A step by step to take a business owner to a brand owner.

How to create raving fans.

How to attract those incredible dream clients.

How to really stand out from the competition.

How to create a brand that looked and felt full of personality.

How to build something that would CONNECT with your audience.

And so for the past three years brand strategy has been at the heart and soul of every brand I have built.

Brand to me is everything.

Branding is your freedom to choose.

It's your golden ticket to the business you dream of running and the clients you dream of working with.

Think of it like this (and forget the cash investment level for a moment).

Let's say you set out to build a car brand. You're starting from scratch and are in the early stages of defining the brand. You can choose to build a low-cost, high-value brand like Ford and sell your cars for £20,000

You can choose to build a high-quality, mid-range brand like Mercedes and sell your cars for £60,000

Or you can choose to be a wildly niche, a super-rich-only brand like Bugatti and sell your cars for £1,000,000+

You don't have to start as Ford and work your way up.

You can decide that your brand will be Bugatti, then create the business model, brand, branding and marketing plan FOR that price range and client.

Elon Musk didn't enter the market with cheap-as-chips Teslas because they were a new concept. He sold them at their worth from day one and yet so many of us have this idea that if we're new, we need to start low and work our way up. Why? You're bringing passion, commitment, hours of practice, and potentially thousands in investments to the table. You're not new -

maybe the business is, but the person behind it is not.

Branding is why I drive four miles and pay over £4 for an Iced Brown Sugar Oat Shaken Espresso at Starbucks.

Branding is why despite being a value shop, we end up spending more money at B&M than we do on the weekly food shop!

Branding is the expectation we have that food from Waitrose will be better than food from Lidl, or a meal at The Ivy will be better than a meal at the local Harvester. It's a standard set and upheld.

And so for small business owners like you, what this does is give us an opportunity.

Opportunity to create a business, a lifestyle and an income that serves us simply by building a brand and THIS is why I am so in love with all things branding and I am super excited that I get to support you on this journey.

Chapter 3
Business, Brand, Branding

Let's start at the foundations and get ourselves super clear on these things. I want the content of this book to INGRAIN itself into your brain and it's only going to do that if we have complete clarity.

For most of us, well probably ALL of us, it's the business that comes first.

We have a thing we want to do.

Something we want to sell.

An idea, a product, an invention.

The functional, 'give me your money and I'll give you XYZ in return' thing that sits at the centre of our business. Then we get excited, grab a logo from somewhere, create some social media accounts and get to work. #bossbabe right?

It's common to think at this point you're building a brand because you're chucking said logo on all the things but actually, what you really have is a business with a logo.

Why is it that when we think 'branding' we think 'logo'? The irony here is, your logo means very little to your audience and forms just a tiny piece of your brand - but let's skim over that for a moment and I'll come back to it.

Let me explain the difference between business, brand and branding.

I have a cool analogy to do this...

(By the way, if you're doing this work now, and feel like you're going back on yourself or that you've 'done things in the wrong order' I promise, you haven't. You are sitting with the rest of us, who got excited, took action and spent some time figuring out how all the pieces fitted together.)

Think of your business as if it were a person - a friend, standing in front of you.

The business is how they function. It's all of the things they 'do' as a human. They need to eat, drink, walk, talk, and poop (sorry) ... it's their physical function. This stuff is imperative to their survival (just like selling selling is essential to the survival of your business) but has zero to do with why you like them or whether you want to be their friend or not.

The brand is their personality. It's all the reasons you love them. It's their sense of humour, their life experiences, their compassion, their empathy, and their kind and caring nature. It's the things about them that draw you in and make you go 'yep, that's my mate and I think she's brilliant'.

The branding is their self-expression. It's the clothes they wear, their hair colour and style, their make-up choices, their shoes, or their choice to have piercings or tattoos. It's all the things that let you know without speaking to them that you two will get along and you've found your person.

As a person, we need all three of these things to be a normal, functioning members of society. If we don't function, we don't survive, if we have no personality, we have no mates, and if we have no clothes well…

My point is, as people we need them all and your business is no different. Yes, you need the functional - if your business doesn't sell anything, it's not going to survive for very long as a business, but we also need the brand so that our audience has a reason to buy from us and we need the branding to communicate to our audience that we might be a brand they'll connect with and enjoy buying from.

Your brand is the very reason people buy from, prioritise, recommend or remain loyal to your business. Your branding is the style, your brand is the substance.

Can you see now how important it is?

The three work together to create a business that attracts new clients, has a strong presence, brings return customers and clients and ideally an army of raving fans who will recommend us to everyone and anyone they meet.

Chapter 4
No new messages

We're skipping a step and jumping straight to your brand. You don't need me to tell you what your business is or what it does. That's not what this book is about, and you've probably already got that figured out. (If not, you might find this work helps you get clear on your mission as a business owner and the impact you are here to make)

So why is building a brand important?

Well, if you're still not on board with the idea that building a brand is a necessary part of building and growing a business then let's look at things in a bit more detail.

In this day and age (that makes me feel old to say) the truly unique businesses are far and few between and most of us are pedalling a been-done-before idea in new packaging. Unless you invented it, or it's some groundbreaking new thing, it's been done before.

There are no new messages, only new messengers.

> Estate agency
> Beauty salons
> Brand Design
> Makeup Artistry
> Personal Trainer
> Candles and Wax Melts

They've all been done before, but that doesn't mean new businesses aren't popping up left, right and centre in these industries, making waves and seeing success.

This is because, well, brand.

They're not necessarily saying or doing anything new - it's the way they're doing or saying it that makes the difference.

The business is not unique, but the BRAND can be.

There is room for all, but to shine, we must embrace our uniqueness.

There are 7 Billion people on this planet each as unique as the next, right? And it stands to reason that each of those 7 billion people would have a slightly different perspective on life and a slightly different way of thinking to the next person.

Sooooo, if the personality and insight of every single business owner is unique then the personality (BRAND) of every single business must also be unique, right?

Sure, personalities can be similar as can brands. But they're never going to be identical and this is where we leverage and stand out.

Take the big five supermarkets as an example. They all sell the exact same products at very similar prices, but all have their place in the market and their way of showing up; their personalities, values and ways of marketing themselves are not the same.

Asda is not Waitrose.

Pepsi is not Coca-Cola.

Ferrari is not Lamborghini.

Each is unique, and so are you.

So Where Do We Begin?

Building a brand is about building a community; finding like-minded people we can connect with, who will then talk about us to the like-minded people they're connected with.

'Customer' is not enough. We want hard-core, raving FANS of our brand.

We want the people who will sing our praises to all and sundry just because they want to.

Just because they GET what we're doing, see the value of the impact we're able to make and are making, and believe in our message enough that it becomes (or perhaps already is) their message too.

And don't get me wrong - you don't need a ground-breaking message that'll change the world to connect with people, sometimes it's the simplest of things.

You might work with a coach because she's an advocate for body positivity and you have teenage children you're worried about.

You might choose a carbon-neutral business to work with because you value their commitment to the environment.

Or you might book Jessica to cut your hair simply because you love how you're treated when you walk into her salon. You feel like she rolls the red carpet out for you and that time for yourself is the self-care that gets you through a busy month.

These things that run above and beyond the simple transaction are your brand. These are where we create connections and so this is where we need to begin.

What is it about you, or your business that connects with your audience?

I realise this is actually a huge question and probably has you thinking, 'well Rosie, this is the whole reason I bought this book and I'm reading it because I don't know the answers to questions like these.'

So let's take some time to think, and here's some prompts that'll help you dig...

- Think about real life friendships or relationships; what subjects, values or interests do you bond over?
- How do you go over and above for your customers? Why is this important to you?
- Look back at past reviews. What are your clients telling you?
- Look over your past social media content. What gets the most comments or engagement? What do people tag you in?
- Where does your journey to where you are now overlap with your ideal client's journey? Where is the moment you share feelings or emotions?
- How does the life of your ideal client overlap with yours? What interests or values do you share? Are they in a similar point in life as you?

Chapter 5
Think, then do

Brand Strategy is a term that gets thrown around a lot - I've chucked it in here a few times so let's dig deep into what it means, what it covers and why it's so important.

Put really simply,

'Brand Strategy is the thinking that comes before the doing'

We've established it's the Brand that's doing all the heavy lifting for you, and it's the process of Brand Strategy that helps us to define what that brand is. It sounds complicated, but really, it's just a bunch of questions with the answers compiled into a few sentences that give us the clarity we need to then do things like write copy, plan content and create your visuals.

Brand Strategy includes:

- Your brand story
- Mission
- Values
- Vision
- Client Experience
- Tone of Voice
- Personality
- Positioning
- Culture
- Behaviours

This information helps us to determine things like:

What is it that makes us unique?

Where our values overlap with our client's values

What we should name our business

How we should name products or offers

Our big goals and how our brand will help us achieve them

Where we sit in the market against our competitors

Our core message

What our visual branding (brand identity) needs to communicate

These words still sound a little 'industry' so let me break them down for you.

Your Brand Story - this is how your business came to be. Often your own personal journey. Where did the inspiration come from? What problem were you solving? How did you get your offer/service/product to market?

This isn't just a useful tool when it comes to connecting with your audience, this is also where things like website copy and social media content come from.

Mission - What do you do? Who do you serve? How do you serve them?

Values - Same as any living person, what's important to you? What do you advocate for? What are your hard no's and on the flip side, what is a non-negotiable standard for you? Where do you set your boundaries?

Vision - What does the future look like? What impact do you want to make on your industry or the world? What are you trying to change, improve or become?

Client Experience - Fairly straightforward - how do you serve your clients? What about their experience with you is different? Maybe you offer something no one else does, you do it differently or maybe you just do it more thoroughly. Maybe you send welcome gifts, Christmas cards, and personal messages - how does working with you feel better/different to working with someone else?

Tone of Voice - Sits alongside personality. How do you speak? Is your language formal? Direct? Simple? Quirky?

Personality - Includes tone of voice but this applies to the brand as a whole rather than just voice and language. Are you fun and playful? Innovative and forward-thinking? Meticulous and thoughtful? Maybe you're a whole combination of things!

Positioning - Where do you sit in your market? High end? Value? Authentic? Casual? Mainstream? Unique? Edgy?

Brand Culture - This is how your brand values are translated throughout your business, down to employees and how they interact with your clients (this is more valuable for larger brands but important as you start to scale)

Behaviours - This is how you act and show up. For example, maybe 'community' is a value of your brand - this means your behaviours will be things like high touch courses, retreats, showing up personally at local events rather than courses that are completely self-study and sending out mass mailshots.

Chapter 6
Your Story

This is where I always begin with my clients. Your story and journey to where you are today are ALWAYS important. It's really common to think it isn't that because nothing wildly dramatic has happened along the way that it's not worth sharing but I promise you it is.

Maybe you felt unfulfilled in a previous role and left to find freedom.

Maybe you fell into your industry by mistake and it quickly became a passion.

Maybe you needed a more flexible lifestyle around your family.

Maybe you created a product having not been able to find what you were looking for.

Your Story

You read some of my story at the start of this book; was there anything there you connected with? Why?

There is always a reason and always significance to the experiences we have.

It's also worth noting that doing this work often is necessary - or at least being aware of it as your journey develops. You are constantly adding new chapters to your story - overcoming new obstacles, growing, evolving and finding new and relevant things.

For example, the fact that an argument over fonts was the trigger for me to hand in my notice at my 9-5 wasn't relevant at all before becoming a brand designer - but now, it's a funny little anecdote along the way that needs to be highlighted.

My recommendation here is to either write this down or involve a friend. Ideally, if you have friends who also have a business - someone with the right mindset - this will help massively.

(Small plug, you can also book 1:1 with me and we can do this together)

We can't always see for ourselves the things that are relevant to the story. The words or phrases we're repeating along the way. Even as a Brand Strategist myself, it's not always clear what is relevant and what is not, and I need help too! It's one of those 'once you see it' situations, but you need someone to show you first.

Start at the beginning and remember to ask 'why' along the way.

Why did that happen?

Why did you make that decision?

Why did you feel that way?

When I do this with clients, what I'm really on is a journey to understand them. I want to know them, so I dig - I play detective. I ask questions that might not feel relevant at the moment, but just might hold the key to what makes them, 'them' and what will help us to create a brand they're connected to on a soul level.

That's something I like to call wild alignment.

Things like:

> Your story and why things panned out this way for you
> How you spend your time
> How you'd like to spend your time
> How you like to switch off and recharge
> What you do when you're feeling stressed, overwhelmed or in search of inspiration
> What your dream home looks like
> Any rituals or routines you have
> Any home comforts you might take on holiday with you
> The shows you watch and the music you listen to
> The books you read
> Any pets and family you have
> Styles and aesthetics you are drawn to - how you decorate your home/workspace

We need to find and pinpoint your default settings because this is you at your most authentic, and when we can craft a business based on you and the things that light you up, we give you a platform from which to share your message that feels exciting, aligned and authentic.

For example, I have two small children, I've watched the US Office more times than I care to know, and I take my coffee machine on holiday with me (UK breaks only I'm not a complete nutcase) along with my favourite mug. I'm obsessed with beautiful glassware and drink far more water throughout my day if it's in a glass I love. I love clean, simple, timeless design and love to have quality, timeless clothing in my wardrobe (mixed up with the odd flash of leopard print of course).

I love to work in peace and calm, with Lo-fi music, the sound of rain and a candle burning. I'm at my most productive when I work in the early hours of the morning when it feels like the whole world is asleep and I'm free from the pressures of notifications and my inbox.

These are my default settings. I don't have to force or think about any of it - they are what I love, and it flows naturally. I value comfort, experiences and creating peaceful moments of luxury throughout my day. I can romanticise even the simplest things - like shopping for freshly baked bread for my peanut butter and banana on toast in the morning. I'm a strong believer that we are here to spend our time doing something we love, with people we love so a good work/life balance is important to me. People call me the Queen of Boundaries which I love because it means that I've gotten good at saying no! Hahaha.

I am here to attract those who enjoy the same and by design, I repel those who do not. You have no idea how many times I'll mention things like drinking from a fancy glass to my clients and they say, 'OMG same'. It sounds small, but it's an alignment in values and a sign you're attracting the right people.

Chapter 7
What's it all for?

Now we need to work on the rest.

Brand Strategy can be pretty extensive and I'd always recommend, wherever possible, working with an expert to pull all the pieces together, but in the interim, until you have that capital to invest, this book is designed to help you do the hard work yourself.

So next up we're going to work on defining your message, your mission, your vision and your values.

First, though, I want you to think about your story and the things that wind you up.

What are you passionate about that makes you mad?

Where are the injustices in the world that you feel compelled to speak up for?

What experiences have you had that you don't want anyone else to go through?

Take those thoughts with you into this next section of the book...

Your Mission

Your mission is all about what you do, in business. It sounds more complicated than it is, so let me give you an example of the Brand by Design mission statement.

Brand by Design is a full-service brand and design studio that uses Brand Strategy to craft wildly-aligned, scroll-stopping brands for ambitious, heart-led women in business

To write this statement, we need to answer 3 key things:

(For ease, I'll bold out the words that answer each question)

What is your business here to do?

Brand by Design is a full-service brand and design studio that uses Brand Strategy to craft wildly aligned, scroll-stopping brands for ambitious, heart-led women in business

How does it do it?

Brand by Design is a full-service brand and design studio that uses Brand Strategy to craft wildly aligned, scroll-stopping brands for ambitious, heart-led women in business

Who does it do it for?

Brand by Design is a full-service brand and design studio that uses Brand Strategy to craft wildly aligned, scroll-stopping brands for ambitious, heart-led women in business

Your Core Message

The insight you now have into your story will help you write this. Think about the things you need your clients to know, both about you and about themselves. What is something that you wish more people understood?

Let's look at the Brand by Design core message:

Brand Strategy is the key to building a brand that feels like you, so you can step out with confidence, create a brand that gets you seen, heard and loved, and in turn create a lifestyle that serves you

A huge part of my personal journey is around creating a business that serves my needs as much as my clients and showing my audience that you get to have all the things.

For example, right now, I'm writing this in a cafe in my favourite part of town. I've bought myself breakfast (the streaky bacon on sourdough toast sandwich I've been craving for about a week) and now I'm sipping an Americano while Micheal Buble Christmas songs play. My view out the door is of two of the biggest superyachts I've ever seen. I built this. I built this lifestyle on purpose and I believe everyone has the right to create this level of happiness for themselves in their lives.

There is a business out there for everyone.

Brand Strategy is the key that can help you build a business that lights you up and allows you to have the work/life balance you crave.

My boundaries are super strong now. I don't work all the hours - I am as intentional about my time working as I am about my time not working and value my time in rest and recharge mode (If you know Human Design, I'm a Manifestor so this time is essential for me).

Having been a workaholic in the past, I am now firmly anti-hustle and am passionate about showing my clients a different way to work.

What can you see, what do you know, or what do you believe, that the world needs to know about?

Your Vision

While your mission is about what your business does, your message is about what you're here to tell or show the world, your vision is about how you picture the world or the change you're creating.

If everyone heard your message, what would the work look like? How would things be different? What communities or movements are you changing or creating? What cultures are you improving or spreading?

Me, I want to live in a world full of diversity. Where people don't feel tied to one particular way of working; where the corporate mentality is gone, people are free and feel confident to be themselves and in turn are happier, and more productive with a better work/life balance.

I believe that we need to lose the school/college/university/degree/job until we retire and instead create more entrepreneurs and free thinkers. We need more freedom, more trust in our employees and more flexible working options.

Your Core Values

Your values form the core, guiding principles and morality of your business.

Shared values are also a huge part of how we connect with other people. Think about it - as we grow and evolve the superficial stuff like our hobbies often change. These parts of our lives are often circumstantial - for example, maybe dancing was a hobby until you had children and now, finding yourself with less available time, you've switched that for something you can enjoy at home.

If we connect with people over our love of dance, that relationship may dwindle when were no longer in that part of our life.

Our values though, aren't as open to change over time. I'm not saying they can't change as you do, but it's usually a case of adding new as we experience new things, rather than getting rid of old.

Let's define some of our core values.

> Where do your boundaries lie?
> What's the minimum standard for you in your business?
> What's something you always do?
> What's something you'd never do?
> What's something you'd decline a client for?
> What do you believe in?
> What do you prioritise?

A useful exercise is to think about it as if you were teaching a member of staff to work in your business. What do they need to know to meet your standards and support your clients or customers how you would personally?

For example, some Brand by Design's core values are: (You don't need to stick to just 3)

Customer first service

Operating in a client-first mindset. Never placing business needs or interests above that of the client.

At our design studio, we're upfront about what we can and can't do, and we won't take on work that we're not a good fit for or don't have the expertise for. If we think there's a better solution then we'll be honest and tell the client. It's a commitment to providing the best possible outcome and experience, without compromising.

Balance & Sustainability

Instilling healthy boundaries and encouraging our clients to do the same.

Sustainability isn't only for the planet, it's for your well-being too. We believe in having everything you want, but enjoying everything all at once is a surefire way to burn out. We prioritise balance and flexibility, and we guide our clients to do the same through effective communication, upholding our own boundaries, through our one to one work and through resources such as this one that explain how to use Brand Strategy to build a brand and business that serves you.

Transparency & Integrity

We don't do weird ambiguous pricing or sneaky hidden costs, we don't do pushy sales calls or chase for bookings or clients, and hold ourselves accountable for the quality of our work.

So what do I do with this information?

Everything.

You do everything with this information.

I'm not even joking. What you've done there is create the very foundations, the core, the biological DNA of your business. You've defined what you're here to do, who it's for and why it matters to the world. You've crafted a strong message and so now we need to share it - clearly, consistently, over and over.

From this information you can:

- Create a scroll-stopping visual brand identity
- Write website copy that converts
- Plan brand photoshoots
- Hire staff
- Plan out courses, products and offers
- Name your business (if you haven't already)
- Write a clear marketing strategy
- Map out your content and choose your social media platforms effectively

I'm sure there's more to this list but we'll leave it there for a minute. My next step with a client is typically to move into brand visuals so let's talk about that...

Chapter 8
Scroll-Stopping Visuals

It's entirely possible that you picked up this book about 'branding' and thought it was 7000 words about colour palettes and logos yet here you are more than 6000 words in thinking 'she's not mentioned a single thing about branding yet'

Or maybe not. It depends on where you are in your business/brand/branding journey I think.

It's funny isn't it how most often when we think of branding our heads go straight to logos. Why is that? I mean, I'm guilty of it too! When I came into the design industry initially, I was making £29 logos. No strategy - just roll up, tell me what you want and get the job done.

It was all style but no real substance. Beauty, but no brains.

Up until that point I'd spent three years in network marketing. I was very clear on what branding meant to me, but while I was consciously competent in creating my own personal brand, I didn't have any real understanding of the depth and magnitude at which a brand needs to influence your branding.

Let's talk about branding and look at what that includes:

- Your logo
- Your colour palette
- Your font choices
- Patterns
- Icons or brand marks
- Illustrations
- Brand Photographer
- Layouts
- Style and Aesthetic

Think of your visual brand like a puzzle. You need all the pieces to match up to create the right big picture. You can't pinch one from another puzzle and hope it'll fit, nor can you complete the picture if you have one missing.

But you can also see how all the responsibility isn't resting on just one thing

i.e. it's not resting on just your logo to do all the work. You're creating a visual identity that is recognisable through a whole bunch of different elements.

Let's translate

So we've done the Strategy work and we know who we are, what we're here to do, and how we're going to make an impact.

Now, we need a visual brand that communicates all of that without actually saying any of it.

Eh?

Our worlds are filled with assumptions, connotations and visual references. We make judgements on things like quality, value, experience, and values based on what we see; the colours used, layouts, aesthetic styling etc.

We need to work out what all this strategy work LOOKS like on paper.

What colours is it?
What fonts is it?
What does our brand photography look like?
What does our logo need to represent?
What does our style need to do for us?

The first step to this is creating a list of adjectives. Usually, I'll note these down as I'm listening to a client talk to me about their business, their work or their clients. I'll write down those keywords that help me build a picture of who they are and the impact they are making.

To start with, choose any you feel apply to you and your brand. You can ask someone to help you if you feel like it would help. You can also go and ask your audience on your social media!

(This list is by no means exhaustive of course - feel free to add your own)

> Active
> Adorable
> Adventurous
> Ambitious
> Artistic

Athletic
Alternative

———

Bold
Brave

———

Calm
Caring
Casual
Charming
Cheerful
Chic
Classic
Clever
Collaborative
Comfortable
Confident
Conservative
Contemporary
Convenient
Cool
Cooperative
Courageous

Cutting Edge
Creative
Custom

———

Dazzling
Debonair
Delicate
Delightful
Detailed
Determined
Direct
Dramatic
Dynamic

———

Eager
Earthy
Eccentric
Efficient
Elegant
Enchanting
Endearing
Energetic
Ethereal

Exciting
Exuberant

———

Fabulous
Familiar
Fashionable
Festive
Fierce
Flirty
Formal
Frank
Fresh
Friendly
Fun
Functional
Funny
Futuristic
Feminine

———

Generous
Gentle
Glamorous
Graceful

Hip
Hilarious
Historic

Impactful
Industrial
Informal
Innovative
Inspiring
Intense
Intentional
Inviting
Irreverent

Jolly
Joyous

Low Maintenance
Lively

Lush

———

Majestic
Mature
Modern

———

Natural
Nifty
Noisy
No-nonsense
Nostalgic

———

Organic

———

Plain
Playful
Plucky
Powerful
Professional

Proud

―――

Quaint
Quirky

―――

Radiant
Rebellious
Reflective
Relaxing
Reliable
Retro
Revolutionary
Romantic
Rustic

―――

Scholarly
Secure
Sensitive
Serious
Silly
Sincere

Sleek
Smart
Soothing
Sophisticated
Stable
Stimulating
Striking
Strong
Stunning
Stylish
Sustainable
Swanky

———

Timeless
Tranquil
Trustworthy

———

Unconventional
Urban

———

Versatile

Vintage

———

Whimsical
Wild
Witty
Wistful

———

Youthful

Now you have your list, we're going to try and narrow it down to maybe five or six. To do this, look at where you might be able to group words.

For example, you might have:

Powerful
Confident
Bold

You could probably just use Bold to surmise all of these.

We're trying to create a vibe here. A feeling that we will then look to create in our audience when they see our content.

Now you have your list, we're going to start with colours and font choices, and we're going to base these on psychology.

I'm not going to deep dive into actually creating a visual brand with you, because if you're doing this ahead of working with a designer, they will explore this with you but if you're about to DIY your branding or just want more of an insight into what your visual brand is (or isn't) doing for you then this next section will be ideal.

You can do this one of two ways. We're going to match up our adjectives to the colour palette we're using.

We need around five colours in our palette. These should be a mixture of contrasting and complementary shades. For example, you need contrasting colours that work one on top of the other, and complimentary colours that work with each other. You can use more than one shade within the same colour, for example, light blue and dark blue, light pink and dark pink.

I want you to jump into Google...

If you already have a colour palette and want to check if it's right, then google '*insert colour* meaning colour psychology'

If you don't or you're starting from scratch, google 'colour psychology meaning *insert adjective*'

Make some notes of the answers you get and do this for all the colours/adjectives you have. You can also jump into something like Pinterest and type in 'adjective and adjective colour palettes' and it'll throw a bunch of ideas at you. You can use Canva to help define the actual colours you want to use, making sure you make a note of the HEX code (this is the little 6-digit code each colour has). You can use this # to replicate your exact colours.

Next up is fonts.

Your choice of fonts says a lot more than we physically say.

Different styles of fonts can be used to communicate different values and aesthetic styles.

This is a Serif Font

Serif fonts are classic and traditional (think Newspaper print) and so bring that feeling of respectability and trust. The word 'serif' actually refers to the little flicks on the ends of the letters (circled). These fonts are great to position you as an expert and create authority in your industry. If quality, heritage or luxury are values of yours, a Serif could be a great choice.

This is a Sans Serif Font

In contrast, Sans Serif literally means 'without Serif' and so these fonts are recognisable by their simple, minimalist designs. These fonts are clean, modern and easy to read and ideal if you want to create a feeling of calm, simplicity or clarity for your audience. Perfect for 'we make xyz simple' brands.

This is a Script font

Script fonts add personality and flair to your brand and are great if you want your brand to feel friendly, informal or personal. They can be hard to read though and aren't really suitable for large amounts of text so it's best to pair them with a Serif or Sans Serif. Think of them like a signature, accent or decoration and use them sparingly for the most impact. Also, remember they're meant to reflect hand-writing, so try not to use them in all caps - it just looks weird.

Pairing contrasting fonts works well and also means you can lean into the right styles for those different adjectives. For example, you might be Modern but Chic - in which case you might choose a Vogue like Serif alongside a super minimal Sans Serif.

Choose two ideally, or three if you want to pick one from each style. For the serif and sans serif, look for styles that have multiple weights (for example, regular, bold, italic) so you have a little more flexibility in how you're using them.

Never pair two from the same category together - it'll just look like you don't know what you're meant to be using. We need contrast between them, but also, each font style serves its purpose to speak for your brand. Either choose one style and use it for everything, or one from each category.

For your logo, I want to stress that representation, not illustration is key.

It doesn't need to be a picture of what you do.

It does need to represent who you are.

My recommendation, if you're going to DIY your branding, is to keep it simple.

Choose a font (or combination of fonts) that works for your brand and just write the name of your business in one or a mixture of those fonts.

It can be that simple, since your fonts, colour palette, messaging and photography are also doing the work.

Remember, branding is all of the following:

- Logos
- Colour palette
- Font choices
- Aesthetic style
- Layouts
- Graphics
- Website design and usability
- Print collateral and finishes
- Brand photography
- Product photography
- Stock imagery

Once we're clear on the visual brand, things like creating graphics for your social media become a million times easier. If you know you always use X font, your logo always sits on the top left corner, and your contact info is at the bottom, then you can whip through a bunch of content super quickly.

If you know you have certain props that represent your personality and your business, you can feature them in every brand photo. It'll help you choose outfits and locations for shoots. Even down to how you have things like business cards printed. I LOVE texture, so we use it in my brand photos, but I also have my business cards printed on recycled cotton cards, because it gives them a high-end feel and an unusual finish.

This year, I'll be ticking off a huge business goal and moving into an office to build my design studio - EVEN the location of the studio needs to be on brand - does the area fit with my brand style and values?

Chapter 9
Come work with me

I feel like branding comes with this kind of catch-22 scenario for lots of business owners. You've got to invest to make the money, but you need the money to invest!

What I will say is this... having some skin in the game will get you a better result. (This goes for all of the things by the way, not just your branding and the same applies to your clients and customers - even a tiny payment is better than no payment)

How much skin is relative to what's available, but I would always recommend pushing yourself to the edge of what feels comfortable.

My first investment in my business was on a payment plan at £97 a month. I honestly could have thrown up after hitting the sign-up button, but that knowledge changed my business and as things have grown, so has what feels comfortable and so have the investments.

Let me run you through some of my favourite offers right now... (depending on when you bought/are reading this book, these may change so head to my website to check)

Brand In A Day

This offer is a favourite of mine too purely because of its simplicity. You would be amazed at what can be done in a day. It's an ideal package if you're in a hurry or on a budget and is a great next step if you've done the work in this book as we've been going along.

Over a single day, we work collaboratively through open communication to devise a strategy, create a cohesive brand concept and deliver on typography, logo designs, and brand guidelines.

This package gets you the unique, strategic, professional brand identity you need without the larger investment.

At the end of the project you'll receive all your logo files, along with a simple brand guidelines document that outsides your font choices and how to use them, along with your colour palette.

If you'd prefer to take a little more time over your branding or want a more comprehensive experience then we have larger packages that can include social media branding, print collateral and promotional items, website design, or brand photography then go take a look on the Brand by Design website.

The Power Hour

If you've reached this point of the book thinking ok, this is great but I could do with a hand to put it all together then a power hour is a great place to start. We can jump on a zoom or grab a coffee if you're local to me and start from the start. You can book one, or a block of calls to really take a deep dive. I also offer a half day workshop hosted over Breakfast as well as a 12 month package to keep you accountable while you build your brand.

Again, take a look on the Brand by Design website and fill out the enquiry form to get in touch and we'll see what option works best for you.

The Sweet Retreat

The wild card - but a super special offer that'll take you far deeper on a journey of connection with yourself. The retreat is an offer I run in collaboration with another brand and business development expert. It's three nights in a nothing short of stunning house in the Brecon Beacons in Wales. Workshops, guest experts, gifts and surprises, a mini session with our brand photographer and time for yourself.

Supporting you not just in your brand, but in creating an intentional and successful year ahead of you.

You can stay in a private suite, or share with a business bestie and receive a discount. You'll need to head to the Brand by Design website for the full details.

Here's hoping that this little book has given you a well-needed insight into your brand, and how you can create something that looks and feels wildly aligned with you, and connects with your audience.

If we're not already connected, I'd love to hear what you thought - reach out to me on social media and let me know.

Add me as a friend on Facebook: Rosie Wilkins

Follow me on Instagram: @_brandbydesign

Visit my website: www.brandby-design.com

Acknowledgments

I feel incredibly blessed to be at the point in my journey where writing a book like this is even possible, and so I can't let the moment pass without saying thank you to the people who have been there while it came to life. Rosie Wilkins, in PRINT! Imagine that!

Guy. I wouldn't be here without you. For everything you are and everything you do - thank you for being my rock, my biggest believer, for trusting in me and for putting up with my impulsiveness!

My mum, for always being there, unconditionally; and my Dad, who is no longer with us but a constant reminder that life is short, retirement isn't guaranteed and finding happiness in today is key.

My beautiful girls, thank you for being my reason to grow. You have challenged me in every way possible and while I know I won't always be perfect, you make me want to be better than I was yesterday.

Nicola, for being an epic business partner through the conception of Brand by Design and for introducing me to Human Design. You changed my life and gave me the permission slip I needed to just be me.

Lily and Hannah, my studio buddies, for helping me take Brand by Design to it's next level and lighting up my work days with laughter, coffee and croissants (and the occasional emotional support!)

JoJo Smith, for bringing pink sassy joy to my life the moment you appeared in my inbox back in 2019. You are my reminder to push myself outside of my comfort zone and to focus on the fun!

Louis, you absolute Cephalopod, thank you for the extensive voice notes, comprehensive analysis and willingness to fight my corner.

Printed in Dunstable, United Kingdom